# THE *Brave* Little *Soldier*
## WHO JUST WOULDN'T DIE

Kevin L. Tennyson

Trilogy Christian Publishers
A Wholly Owned Subsidiary of Trinity Broadcasting Network
2442 Michelle Drive
Tustin, CA 92780
Copyright © 2024 by Kevin L. Tennyson
All Scripture quotations, unless otherwise noted, are taken from THE HOLY BIBLE, NEW INTERNATIONAL VERSION®, NIV® Copyright © 1973, 1978, 1984, 2011 by Biblica, Inc.® Used by permission. All rights reserved worldwide.
Scripture quotations marked nlt are taken from the Holy Bible, New Living Translation, copyright © 1996, 2004, 2015 by Tyndale House Foundation. Used by permission of Tyndale House Publishers, Inc., Carol Stream, Illinois 60188. All rights reserved.
Scripture quotations marked tlb are taken from The Living Bible copyright © 1971. Used by permission of Tyndale House Publishers, a Division of Tyndale House Ministries, Carol Stream, Illinois 60188. All rights reserved.
Scripture quotations marked (KJV) are taken from The Holy Bible, King James Version. Cambridge Edition: 1769.
All rights reserved, including the right to reproduce this book or portions thereof in any form whatsoever.
For information, address Trilogy Christian Publishing
Rights Department, 2442 Michelle Drive, Tustin, CA 92780.
Trilogy Christian Publishing/ TBN and colophon are trademarks of Trinity Broadcasting Network.
For information about special discounts for bulk purchases, please contact Trilogy Christian Publishing.

Trilogy Disclaimer: The views and content expressed in this book are those of the author and may not necessarily reflect the views and doctrine of Trilogy Christian Publishing or the Trinity Broadcasting Network.

10 9 8 7 6 5 4 3 2 1
Library of Congress Cataloging-in-Publication Data is available.
ISBN 979-8-89333-630-6
ISBN 979-8-89333-631-3

# DEDICATION

This book is dedicated to the loving memory of my wife, Patricia Diane Tennyson (PD).

# ACKNOWLEDGMENTS

To my sister, Kathleen: thank you for your many significant editorial contributions early on in this process.

To my granddaughter, Megan: the many visits to my house during the writing of this book were always cheerful and pleasant. Thank you for staying the course with me, even though you were sworn to secrecy about this book.

To my sister-in-law, Tracy Earnest: Thank you for your significant contributions in retelling your family history. You were with PD her whole life, through the best and the worst of times.

To my dear friend, Ed Wycoff, UCF Professor Emeritus: you were willing to see the manuscript at its worst so that we could bring it to its very best. Your encouragement was second to none, and I am most thankful for your time and professional opinion during this entire process.

# FORWARD

"At one point I seriously began to seriously death."

Against all medical opinions, countless hospital visits, diagnoses, painful procedures, and tests, everyone was certain she wouldn't make it. But against all odds, Patricia Diane Tennyson, or "PD," not only survived, but she thrived and persevered year after year. She fought like a warrior, and her life was a testament to her strength and vigor. This is why she became known as "The Brave Little Soldier Who Just Wouldn't Die."

When the Roe v. Wade Supreme Court ruling was set into motion in 1973, a fire was stoked within Patricia Diane Tennyson (PD), and despite her many physical trials, she was driven by her love of helping women in need. She was the silent leader who was the catalyst for creating a safe-haven and rehabilitation program in Orlando for pregnant women from all walks of life.

Despite long and difficult hospital stays and a lifetime full of physical and unending pain, PD partnered with a few other organizations and charities to move the needle in changing the process of how pregnant women are treated and taken care of. So, she made it her mission to be the voice and the activist for change for these helpless women. Over the years, she helped nearly eighty-eight pregnant women by providing either food, shelter or a loving, warm environment. She knew that it was her unique gifting and life calling to help these girls.

This book will help you gain the understanding through PD's story that regardless of the mountain in front of you, you can overcome anything with faith, strength, hope, and love.

Getting to know the woman behind this story, the realities of her life growing up, facing pain and overcoming it is critical. But even more, understanding her reliance on the Lord through it all gives us a practical roadmap for life. The background of Patricia's life is just the beginning of her legacy for it still lives on today through the lives that she touched.

—Megan

# INTRODUCTION

I am honored to have Kevin Tennyson as my grandfather and to watch our relationship blossom over the past few years through working on this book together. Through this experience, we have gone from family to partners in ministry. Since the passing of his wife, my grandmother, Patricia Diane Tennyson, I have watched him grow in his relationship with Jesus to the place where his heart burns with the desire to go deeper in the knowledge of the beauty of the Lord. He has made it his mission to ensure that her legacy of miracles lives on through this story.

This writing has the intrinsic ability to touch the heart of any reader, because the woman behind this story, the realities of her life growing up, facing pain and overcoming, become personal to you. I found myself many times putting myself in PD's shoes, asking myself the questions, "Would I have chosen this path? Would I have responded to the pain in the same way in these circumstances?" This book offers both first and second person accounts of medical miracles (as well as the events that PD helped launch new approaches in the way Orlando cares for pregnant women).

Kevin gives readers a glimpse into PD's reliance on the Lord throughout all her trials and gives us a practical roadmap for life. But the background of Patricia's life is just the beginning of her legacy, for it still lives on today through the lives that she touched. This book helped me see how life, and the way we choose to live it, can impact the lives of those around us. PD's story is one of the most beautiful examples of how, despite mountains to overcome, one can conquer most anything with hope, strength, and faith.

I will never be able to fully repay my grandfather for the life-altering experience that collaborating on this book has given me. I am confident that each reader will feel convicted to do more in his or her life, be compelled to take action for God's Kingdom, and will elevate his or her faith after reading this book. The life lessons of long suffering, self-sacrifice, and righteousness through my grandmother's story are ones that I will carry forever. Papa, I thank you for being brave enough to come face-to-face with your grief and to choose to carry on by writing about PD's miraculous story so it can be shared with the world.

—Megan

# TABLE OF CONTENTS

DEDICATION . . . . . . . . . . . . . . . . . . . . . . . . . . . . . . 5

ACKNOWLEDGMENTS . . . . . . . . . . . . . . . . . . . . . 7

FORWARD . . . . . . . . . . . . . . . . . . . . . . . . . . . . . . 9

INTRODUCTION . . . . . . . . . . . . . . . . . . . . . . . . . 11

THE ROAD UP FROM HELL . . . . . . . . . . . . . . . . . . 17

    Family History of Heroism . . . . . . . . . . . . . . . . . . . 19
    Satan Launches His Invasion . . . . . . . . . . . . . . . . . 21
    The Fight Begins . . . . . . . . . . . . . . . . . . . . . . . . . . 23
    Questioning Life, Even God . . . . . . . . . . . . . . . . . . 23
    A Deathly Visitation . . . . . . . . . . . . . . . . . . . . . . . 25
    Loss of Living, Looks, and Love . . . . . . . . . . . . . . 26

THEN GOD... . . . . . . . . . . . . . . . . . . . . . . . . . . . . 31

    The Presence of Jesus . . . . . . . . . . . . . . . . . . . . . . 32
    He Gave Me His Love,
    and Then a New Love . . . . . . . . . . . . . . . . . . . . . . 32
    The Peace That Passes All Understanding . . . . . . . . 33
    Eye Witness Account of Divine Love—Kevin's
    Testament . . . . . . . . . . . . . . . . . . . . . . . . . . . . . . 34

FIGHTING THE GOOD FIGHT
BY REACHING OUT . . . . . . . . . . . . . . . . . . . . . . . 37

    Blind Date Opened My Eyes . . . . . . . . . . . . . . . . . 38

PD's Enduring Spark of Energy . . . . . . . . . . . . . . . 39
A Ministry Is Born as Love Returns . . . . . . . . . . . . . 41
Decision to Share Life Together and Be
Part of Her Story . . . . . . . . . . . . . . . . . . . . . . . . . . . . 43
Period of Adjustment . . . . . . . . . . . . . . . . . . . . . . . . 45
New Beginnings:
Building a Home . . . . . . . . . . . . . . . . . . . . . . . . . . . . 46

IMPOSSIBLE STRUGGLE DESPITE THE ODDS . . . . 49

Seeing Through Faith . . . . . . . . . . . . . . . . . . . . . . . . 51
The Long Road of Setbacks . . . . . . . . . . . . . . . . . . . 52
The Torturous Rehab. . . . . . . . . . . . . . . . . . . . . . . . . 54
A Homecoming: But Little Good News . . . . . . . . . . 56
God Honored Me to Help Her Cope. . . . . . . . . . . . . 57
The Heartbreak of Dialysis . . . . . . . . . . . . . . . . . . . 58
Incredible Grace Under Withering Fire . . . . . . . . . . 60

HER GREATEST TREASURE: GREATEST LOSS . . . . 63

Train Up a Child in the Way He Should Go . . . . . . . 64
The Glory of Motherhood, Despite the Challenges . . 65
Theron. . . . . . . . . . . . . . . . . . . . . . . . . . . . . . . . . . . . . 66
Derek. . . . . . . . . . . . . . . . . . . . . . . . . . . . . . . . . . . . . . 68
Jared . . . . . . . . . . . . . . . . . . . . . . . . . . . . . . . . . . . . . . 70
Brandon. . . . . . . . . . . . . . . . . . . . . . . . . . . . . . . . . . . . 73
The Amazing Case of Ronalee "Roni" . . . . . . . . . . . 76

OPENING HER HEART AND HER HOME:
PD'S MINISTRY OF LOVE . . . . . . . . . . . . . . . . . . . . . 81

Saving Rachel . . . . . . . . . . . . . . . . . . . . . . . . . . . . . . 84

A Struggle with the Spirits of Abortion . . . . . . . . . . 86
Love Makes the Difference. . . . . . . . . . . . . . . . . . . 89
Beginning a Rededication to Life . . . . . . . . . . . . . . . 91
Center is Born: Under PD's Quiet Leadership . . . . . . 92
The Beginnings of a Legacy for Life . . . . . . . . . . . . 93
PD: "Only a Vessel Used by Him" . . . . . . . . . . . . . . 93

BENEDICTION FOR A SAINT. . . . . . . . . . . . . . . . . 97

Telling Scars . . . . . . . . . . . . . . . . . . . . . . . . . . . . 98
Importance of a Thankful Heart . . . . . . . . . . . . . . . 99
Others Before Self. . . . . . . . . . . . . . . . . . . . . . . . 100
PD Finally Finds Peace. . . . . . . . . . . . . . . . . . . . . 103

ABOUT THE AUTHOR. . . . . . . . . . . . . . . . . . . . . 107

HIGHLIGHTS OF THE BRAVE LITTLE SOLDIER. . 109

# 1

# THE ROAD UP FROM HELL

*PD in Israel*

*Doctors had given up all hope, yet unbelievably, once again, she opened her eyes*

*and smiled. The medical team
said, "What a fighter!" The
hospital staff got to know
her as "OUR BRAVE LIT-
TLE SOLDIER WHO JUST
WOULDN'T DIE."*

Bill and Patricia Earnest of Atlanta were not unlike other young couples picking up the pieces after World War II in 1945. Bill's experience was made somewhat different since he had to endure a hero's welcome by the city of Atlanta as a notable fighter pilot.

During his last semester at Georgia Tech, Bill was drafted into the Army Air Corps as a pilot officer and immediately distinguished himself with military actions in England, Egypt, and Sicily. In one battle, the squadron Bill led lost eight of its thirteen fighter aircraft.

Legendary General, George Patton, witnessed Bill's phenomenal courage for himself when, during the invasion of Sicily, Bill dove his aircraft through intense enemy fire to destroy four German machine-gun nests on four separate occasions. Patton immediately ordered that Lt. Earnest be awarded the Distinguished Flying Cross for heroism, fourth only to the Congressional Medal of Honor.

Bill's display of an incredible array of traits—the strength of will, daring, determination, and toughness were stunning. But away from the battlefield, the young Earnest family had to re-focus on traits necessary to rebuild their post-war country and loving home.

# FAMILY HISTORY OF HEROISM

It was an unusual time in the U.S. Building a nation starts with rebuilding homes—and rebuilding homes starts with building a family. Like many growing a large family during those days, the Earnests concentrated on hard work. As they settled down, they were blessed with five wonderful children. Their firstborn was a little girl they named Patricia Diane, whose nickname befit her small frame. She became known as simply "PD." PD was a favorite among her extended family. She was close to her grandmothers and aunts and was fascinated by stories of her family, including a grandfather who taught electrical engineering and a grandmother who was a professor of mathematics at Georgia Tech.

PD came from an unusual family of fighters and military officers dating back to the Civil War. Both grandfathers and grandmothers served in World War I, and her father and uncle served in WWII. PD's aunt was one of two women to become an air traffic controller during WWII, and she was the first woman to supervise a high-density tower of air traffic controllers.

Folks probably wondered about the future of this petite and fragile child being born into such a tough and impressive family of soldiers. Certain personality traits in a child often appear to be carried over in the disposition of a family member. Research now indicates that one's genes and environment are intertwined, so both nature and nurture may be involved in our ultimate makeup. But PD's family ties must have had people guessing.

How could this diminutive young girl ever be expected to prove herself on the battlefield of life, coming from such a notable bloodline? Well, she did. But not in the way one would expect. She did it spiritually, through suffering, and with the love of God. It is impossible to read through these pages without seeing the enormous strength of her character. Did that come from PD's lineage of courageous ancestry? We will leave that up to you, the reader, and to researchers.

PD attended Catholic grade schools in Atlanta and Moultrie, Georgia until her dad was once again called upon by the military, this time to train fighter pilots at Spence Air Force Base, Moultrie. She loved growing up in a small town and was extremely popular in high school. But once again, seeing better opportunities, her family moved to Florida. After high school, PD attended Florida State University to major in journalism. She revealed a special gift for writing and even won a class award for storytelling. Sadly, PD was forced to leave FSU when, out of the blue, she became quite ill. It was the beginning of a disease that would become her long-lasting nightmare.

## SATAN LAUNCHES HIS INVASION

In her own words, PD tries to describe the indescribable. She looks back on her earlier attack by this ghastly malady that few had ever known with savagery few have ever encountered:

"Once in a while, the memory of those two years of horror comes slithering back into my present. I gazed at the bleeding, mutilated creature that was somehow me and recalled the relentless pain and terror of that time. Again, I taste the screams rising in my throat. Yet, I am able to revisit this hellish scene with a certain detachment, as if it were a childhood nightmare now outgrown, or something that had happened in another lifetime altogether—as indeed, it had. I had been praying without full commitment in Sunday-to-Sunday lip service to God for all of my twenty-nine years.

"Then, without warning, my long-dormant Crohn's disease awoke and erupted. In the ten years since my doctors discovered the intestinal ulcers, my life had been ordinary; some days good, some days not, and God was in His heaven doing whatever He did there. I was running my own show.... Until...

"In cozy contentment, a warm little toddler snuggled beside me, I fell asleep that drowsy, golden spring afternoon. I never imagined that within an hour, THAT life, for me, would be forever gone. I awoke shuddering on the fringes of Hell, with a flaming fever and the agony of ruptured, abscessed intestines. The hospital was specially prepared as we raced across town.

"I seemed to have been swallowed by a boiling inferno, which consumed the moisture from each cell and scorched my brain. Violent chills accompanied the fever and my body jerked and convulsed so frantically that many strong hands were needed to restrain me under a blanket of ice. My temperature leaped to 108 blazing degrees as the venomous infection snaked throughout my bloodstream.

"My intestines had abscessed and ruptured, spilling poison throughout my body. My family was notified. The experts agreed I would be dead before morning. They decided to operate even though the damage to my body was considered beyond repair and my brain was unquestionably destroyed by the fever. There was little hope. After six grizzly hours of trying to piece back together the massively damaged tissue of my intestinal tract, the surgeon reported: 'Well, she's still alive.' But he was astonished when I regained consciousness, smiled, and greeted him by name.

"'Unbelievable!' other surgeons would say with subsequent surgeries. 'What strength!' 'Such power!' 'What a fighter!' echoed through other recovery rooms after more surgeries. In the months that followed, my reputation spread to every corner of the hospital. Switchboard operators, janitors, security guards, nurses from every floor, EVERYONE came by to look at and pat 'the brave little soldier who just wouldn't die.'"

## THE FIGHT BEGINS

"For the next two years, I battled the overwhelming destruction of my body and soul. The intestines refused to heal, and the abscesses continued to form and rupture, polluting my system with their toxic flow. The abdominal incision gaped open; no sutures could hold together the deteriorated tissue. The alarmingly high fevers soared, and the surgeons repeatedly operated to remove nearly thirty feet of intestines, bit by diseased bit.

"Blood and acidic drainage endlessly pumped from the open incision, melting the skin and eating into my scorched flesh that burned with flaming intensity. Month after month, I screamed inside in torment, but no one ever heard; I kept silent. My pride was such that I refused to admit how much I was suffering or how terrified I was. Whimpering and complaining were for weaklings. I carefully hid my growing desperation and the continuous howling of my soul. Every conscious moment, with my pitifully frail and failing endurance, I constantly chanted, 'I can take it. I can handle it.'"

## QUESTIONING LIFE, EVEN GOD

"My audience mistook my vanity for courage and marveled. Their admiration increased my determination to persevere. But at night, when it was dark and the stage was empty, I openly writhed in agony—and with rage toward the fate that had condemned me. In aching despair, I wept with a yearning for my four little boys.

"At one point I began to seriously consider death. I had never accepted the idea that it could actually happen to me, that it was expected and even inevitable. After deciding not to humiliate myself with a sniveling, whining departure, my thoughts turned to whatever was scheduled to follow. With dread, I began to speculate on the threat of Judgment. For the first time in my life, I recognized the unquestionable existence of God; a fierce, angry God, demanding what I had never been able to achieve: perfection. Reluctantly, I searched inside myself, inspecting my life, trying to discover if I would be acceptable to this fearsome being. As I honestly appraised my own worthiness, I realized, with certainty and a tightening grip of terror, that I had never met His standards. Horrified, I concluded that I was deserving of and undoubtedly destined for Hell! Faced with that unspeakable future, I determined to stay awake; forever, if necessary.

"Overwhelmed with fear and torment, I fought sleep for days, reasoning that I could more effectively battle death while conscious. Vainly I sought help from those around me. Many times, I called for priests to confess my sins, but they provided no peace. I shared my fears with my husband, who scoffed that there was 'nothing beyond the grave and the worms.'

My loving mother patted me and smiled. "What awful things have you ever done to deserve Hell?" No one had the answer, and my anxiety became unbearable. I considered talking to God but had no idea of what to say to make Him change His mind about me. I had never regarded Him as being involved personally with His creatures. His supremacy and awesome power were actually what was so frightening to me about death."

## A DEATHLY VISITATION

"One afternoon, in my mind's eye, I saw a heavy, ominous blackness approaching from the right side of my vision. I watched with fascination as it crept steadily and threateningly into my full frontal view. Suddenly, I understood that it was Death. Within myself, I began to scream in panic, NO! NO! when a brilliant light appeared to my left. This unearthly illumination reached the center of my vision and came against the horrible darkness and pushed it back. For some time, the two pushed against each other, back and forth, receding, progressing, until finally the light prevailed against the darkness and with a mighty thrust, drove it out of sight. For a moment, the radiance just pulsated in my consciousness, then faded, withdrawing. Instinctively, I realized that I had just witnessed a battle between life and death, good and evil; I had just won a reprieve.

"The physical crises were ongoing: I suffered collapsed

lungs and veins, blood clots, heart failure, seizures, hemorrhages, escalated fevers with chills, and always the barbaric, unrelenting pain. My atrophied legs were drawn up in the fetal position, requiring weeks of therapy before being able to walk again. I had become addicted to cortisone and narcotics, and I weighed a mere fifty pounds! Nine operations were performed on me, including a temporary ileostomy (surgery to remove diseased intestines, in which the end portion of the remaining bowel is brought through the abdominal wall, affixed to the skin, and a plastic pouch was attached to collect the drained body waste.) It was to be temporary, and that promise enabled me (barely) to tolerate the disgusting thing."

## Loss of Living, Looks, and Love

"After many critical months of struggling just to stay alive for one more hour, one more day, I was taken off the death watch list. As sighs of relief began to fade, I discovered a new enemy. I began to go blind. The medication to combat Crohn's disease had induced a very rare fungus that destroyed my left eye before anyone noticed and was threatening the right eye as well. An IV was inserted into my jugular vein to administer the fungus-fighting medication. For six interminable weeks, I frantically waited for the verdict.

"Would the treatment be successful, or would I be totally blind? Would I ever see the beautiful faces of my little boys again? Inside, I was like a mindlessly terrified animal caught in a trap. Outside, I kept up the act. Denying the strangling apprehensions, I appeared indomitable, ever brave to accept each fresh assault. The praise and admiration from friends and family continued to pour in, stroking my fiery pride and determination. I could take it. I could even handle blindness.

"My right eye was saved, but my weary, frustrated team of doctors finally ran out of ideas. They recommended specialists in Atlanta, where my parents lived, and I was transferred there. The Atlanta specialists removed my ileostomy, but soon my abdomen rebelled, splitting open in various places and draining acidic waste again on my newly formed skin. After months of wrestling with up to twelve simultaneously erupting and draining fistulae, my bravado began to crack. I became so tired of fighting, discouraged of ever winning again, desperately lonely for my children, concerned over the declining relationship with my husband, and afraid the nightmare would never end. Securing a supply of painkillers and ever-dwindling fortitude, I flew home to the security and support of my family. My baby sat beside me very still, stared at me intently, then solemnly stated, 'You don't LOOK like my "mudder." Also, my husband flatly announced, 'This has been very hard on me. I don't love you anymore.'"

"He convinced me that no judge would award children to a mother too weak and sickly to care for them. Afraid of losing them all in a court battle, realizing that I really couldn't manage four active little boys alone, and convinced that he would change his mind, I reluctantly agreed to divide the boys: two for him and two for me.

"The younger boys and I, practically strangers to each other, moved into a cheap apartment and, too proud to ask for help, struggled to survive on three hundred dollars a month. We were hungry, the boys had nightmares and cried often, and I bitterly grieved over the loss of my first and second sons. The doctor had ordered me to eat nothing for three months: I drank a powdered mixture six times a day instead. This pre-digested diet was to give the intestines a rest, hopefully allowing them time to heal. Although I lived with a gnawing, desperate hunger, the fistulae were blessedly quiet, and I began to hope.

"The joyous day, my first in eighteen months, finally arrived when I was allowed a jar of strained baby applesauce. With tears of happiness rolling down my face, I relished every watery morsel of that heavenly nectar. By the next morning, however, the fistula raged out of control. I returned to Atlanta. By now, all patience was gone. I quit pretending, quit smiling, and quit hoping. The doctors decided that a permanent ileostomy was the answer. The night before surgery, I lay in the bleak darkness of pain, loneliness, and abysmal self-pity. I had finally reached the end of my strength. I had tried so desperately to make it, fought so hard to win, to be brave, and to live. Hopelessly I sobbed, 'It's not fair; there's nothing left for me.'

"I realized that I would never really be well again. I had lost my husband, my sons, my home, my health, and security, my will to live, and tomorrow, my femininity. With an ileostomy, I would be ugly, stinking, deformed, and repulsive. My husband would never want me back. I would forever be dirty and disgusting. No man could ever love me.

"Somberly, I considered the large supply of narcotics in the nightstand and the relief they offered. There was more than enough to provide oblivion. There was no Hell; in fact, to me, living was Hell, and death was my release. Resolutely, I reached for the drawer. My children would not miss me; they had forgotten about me already. My husband did not care. Only my parents, my sister, my family who still loved me... I was such a burden... it would be better this way, I thought. 'Oh, Mother, Daddy.' I groaned, fingering the inviting tablets waiting there for me. 'Please understand. I just can't take this anymore! Oh God, I give up! Oh God, no more...' God? A glimmer of hope sparked within my soul. Desperately, I reached up and cried out, 'OH GOD, HELP ME! PLEASE, HELP ME!'

# 2

# THEN GOD...

*PD in her early school years*

"Instantly, I was caught up in a warmth no human can describe. As God gathered His broken, terrified child and pressed her to His heart, the angry, self-sufficient monster inside was crushed to death. Waves of peace and safety washed over me, then into me, cleansing away the bitter despair of isolation and horror that were consuming. My heart, next to His heart, whispered, 'You're NOT scary, you're wonderful!' 'I'll take care of you.' He promised. 'I love you. I love you.' As He held me, the pain began to subside and gradually disappeared. My heart, throbbing with joy and wonder, seemed to no longer pump mere blood. Instead, racing through my veins was a regenerative power, a force of invincible vitality and new life. In His embrace, the healing process began."

## THE PRESENCE OF JESUS

"At home with my two sons a few months later, while serenely adjusting to my new ileostomy, I met Jesus. I had not really been looking for Him. At that time, I thought my experience with the Father was the ultimate encounter. But suddenly, one midnight, there He was, and there also was His Cross—with a list of MY sins nailed to it. He said, 'This is what Jesus did for you.' Joyous understanding exploded in my brain as the burden of my ruined life dissolved from my soul. I realized that He had saved my life to give me Life, and to set me free from the fear, pain, and the Hell of the incurable, deadly Crohn's disease that had been my road to Calvary."

## HE GAVE ME HIS LOVE, AND THEN A NEW LOVE

"Having my physical and spiritual needs so beautifully provided for, there remained only the fragmentation of my soul. Considering myself unacceptable as a woman, I was trying hard to reconcile myself to the loneliness of single life. Nevertheless, one empty Saturday evening I dared to barely whisper, with no expectations at all, 'Oh, Lord, please send me somebody to love, who will love me.'

"Four days later, He sent Kevin, His very best. Hand-picked by my Father, this precious husband, with much love, has completed the healing and made me whole. The only unresolved heartache I still suffered was the separation from my sons and the grief and anxiety that they did not, at that time, know Jesus. [With their father, a survivalist, they moved three thousand miles away to hide in the mountains from the holocaust they were expecting.] My third son is with them now too. Refusing to come home from a Christmas visit, he complained, 'I can't take any more of that God stuff.' The pain never subsides, but the Lord has given me comfort and hope.

One night as I cried out to Him in sorrow, He vividly made me the promise: "Restrain your voice from weeping and your eyes from tears, for your work, will be rewarded," declares the LORD... there is hope for your descendants... "Your children will return to their own land" (Jeremiah 31:15–17). Then He showed me a vision of all four of them before His throne, reunited with me forever, in Glory."

## THE PEACE THAT PASSES ALL UNDERSTANDING

"God's love is so far beyond our understanding. I was desperate and dying and hurtling towards Hell, so full of rebellious pride and independence, I never once reached out for His outstretched hand. I do not know why He wanted me or why He loved me so much, but He did and was determined to have me for His own. Looking back, I can see the many times He tried to reach me, but I was unreachable. Finally, He had to use emergency procedures to get my attention. God allowed my illness, rejection, and hopelessness, even while He grieved over my stubborn pride that caused it.

> *"One by one, He permitted the sources of my strength to be removed until I could no longer stand alone. When all the substitutes had vanished or been destroyed, and my smug self-sufficiency lay in a mocking heap of rejections all around me, He was there. When finally, I cried out from the pit of my own ego's construction, admitting to my helplessness and need, He held out His arms to me.*
>
> *"He has never let me go. He promises He never will."*
>
> **— Patricia Diane Tennyson**

# Eye Witness Account of Divine Love—Kevin's Testament

This book contains true-life accounts of Faith and Miracles in the life of my beloved wife, Patricia Diane (PD)

Tennyson. It serves as a lasting testament to her memory, as well as to God's unconditional love. PD went to be with her Lord and Savior in Heaven forever on October 24, 2016. The remarkable events in her life history could not have been mere random occurrences. While we might speculate endlessly about their purpose, it is evident that God had something to say to each of us through these events. That will be for each reader to determine.

Until we married in 1977, I had no idea of the incredible horrors and subsequent miraculous interventions into her life by our caring God. During the forty years since, PD's agonizing testimony was painfully revealed to me—on several occasions by her renowned doctor, who called her "a miracle." Her story became bonded into my soul as part of our Christian journey together. Throughout our years of intimate sharing, as a devoted husband and wife, her past travails became part of me. They were also made indelible through my sacred duty of caring for her physically, day by day.

Her testimony came alive to both of us when we were eyewitnesses to PD being blessed even more by repeated God-sent healings after our marriage, which is described in the pages that follow. Therefore, I, Kevin L. Tennyson, do hereby attest to the authenticity of these accounts of Faith and evidence of Miracles without reservation. While I was not included within the enduring agonies and ecstasies of her earlier life's sufferings and healings, I can now confirm, without doubt, that the astonishing accounts of my wife's travails and supernatural healings were altogether true and accurate, as described herein.

# 3

# FIGHTING THE GOOD FIGHT BY REACHING OUT

*PD with daughter in law Judy and granddaughter Jordan*

Her written testimony above reveals to you what happened to her as a result of the deadly and incurable Crohn's disease. Her life expressed how God acted through her tremendous pain and suffering and the miraculous recovery that impacted the lives of others, both locally and nationally. On occasion, she was invited to speak before local churches about God's miraculous healing that had taken place in her life. Churches were crowded, with lines forming at the end of each service as people wanted to thank her personally and even touch her.

# BLIND DATE OPENED MY EYES

I first met PD in the fall of 1977 on a blind date. She was just out of the hospital after many months of surgeries and tremendous suffering—close to two and a half years, including six months of isolation on the death watch list. I had no idea that she was blind in her left eye, had an ileostomy, and had less than four feet of intestines, all as a result of Crohn's disease.

At the time we met, in October, I was finishing a three-year tour of duty as a Company Commander (Drill Instructor) at Orlando's Naval Recruit Training Center. I had orders to leave in December 1977 and report for duty at Norfolk Naval base for six weeks of training with subsequent duty in Italy, reporting aboard the flagship of the U.S. Sixth Fleet, homeported at Giada, Italy.

We enjoyed an especially pleasant date. All we did was talk, but I knew that she was different and that I was in the presence of a real lady. She had warmth, joy, and peace about her that was different from anyone I had ever met. I knew this was a good, kind, and decent person with a very special zest for life. While I was unfamiliar with all of her medical conditions and the extent of her suffering, after our date I knew that I must see her again. Our beautiful evening ended with a simple goodnight hug.

When I returned to the Base that night, I couldn't sleep. I chose to sit outside my barracks, my mind in the clouds, with a smile I couldn't get to go away all night. Not even tired, I felt like I was walking on air. I was twenty-nine years old at the time and had never been married; PD was thirty-two and had four little boys whom she loved passionately.

Her sons were all under the age of ten, and she lived in a small apartment with the two youngest boys, aged five and six; the older boys lived with their father. PD realized she could not manage four active little boys by herself. She had reluctantly agreed to give up the older boys as long as she had unlimited access and rights to them. It saddened her enormously that she was not able to mother the older two children, but she prayed relentlessly for them. Her prayers were heard, for both of these sons turned out to be fine, accomplished men who know the Lord and married godly women. They are good husbands and fathers, and although raised by their father, they remained very close to their mother. Both men loved, honored, and respected her.

## PD's Enduring Spark of Energy

One of the most amazing things about PD's condition was her tremendous amount of energy, even though there did not appear to be anything within her body to produce the iron the blood needs to keep a body alive. Remember, all of her large intestine had been removed along with half of her small intestine, twenty-eight and a half feet in total.

PD's hope in the Lord was unrelenting; her source of strength and drive was a mystery to many. But Isaiah described it perfectly.

> *"Even youths grow tired and weary, and young men stumble and fall, but those who hope in the Lord will renew their strength. They will soar on wings like eagles; they will run and not grow weary, they will walk and not faint" (Isaiah 40:30–31).*

The large intestine, twenty-four feet, is the body's anatomical part that makes the iron for our blood. People missing just a few feet of the large intestine normally have to take B-12 shots weekly and take additional medications to get their blood levels of iron to normal levels. PD's blood was rich in iron and she didn't need shots or medications. Her doctor kept a close eye on her blood work, and the nurse, who loved PD, would call with excitement, praising God every time about the results of her healthy blood reading. An ongoing miracle she was.

Dr. Frank Bone, her gastroenterologist, was renowned in his specialty. He told me he loved PD as if she were his daughter. I asked him once about how her blood could remain rich in iron despite her difficulties. He explained to me privately that when doctors don't have an answer to a patient's problem, they call upon other doctors until they can find an answer. He added that in PD's case, however, there was no one alive to compare her to, and then, with a soft smile, he said that when medical science can't explain it, we call it "a miracle."

Upon his retirement, Dr. Bone wanted to see PD one last time. He embraced her in a precious moment as she thanked him for saving her life. Then, he wanted to show her something; it was his Governors' Award, presented to only the second physician in the history of the state of Florida. This award was for excellence in his practice of medicine for over fifty years.

He was quite proud of the well-deserved honor and wanted PD, especially, to know of the part she played.

> *"Therefore we do not lose heart. Though outwardly we are wasting away, yet inwardly we are being renewed day by day" (2 Corinthians 4:16).*

# A Ministry Is Born as Love Returns

PD's life was spared by God, and her life was forever transformed. She willingly told her story to anyone who asked or wanted to know, since she was not supposed to

THE BRAVE LITTLE SOLDIER WHO JUST WOULDN'T DIE

have lived. But God had other plans for her life. People were amazed at her story, rejoicing and praising God along with her. I finally suggested that she write out her testimony about her life and the healings that had taken place. She did. A few copies were given out and her story went far and wide as churches and news broadcast channels asked her to speak about her life and the miracles. She jumped into telling her story with unbelievable energy. Four medical teaching hospitals called to ask questions before, during, and after hospitalization. Word spread within the church community about PD and her life, and soon a TV station wanted to film her as she told her astonishing story.

The filming was done on the grounds of a large church. I was not there in Orlando that day but was told that all three cameramen had tears in their eyes. The film was aired several times on a Christian TV station, and it touched and inspired the lives of thousands locally.

Not long after, the *700 Club* called from Virginia Beach and asked if they could come down to Orlando to film her testimony, which would be aired nationally in over fifty-five million homes. PD wholeheartedly agreed to the offer. A director came and filmed her story for eight hours at our home and in Orlando hospital. The video producer talked with PD at length. The whole crew asked questions and praised the Lord after hearing about her overcoming all that she had gone through. She never hesitated to share that it was all God's love for her and his healing power that saved her from death many, many times.

Several years earlier, I had the feeling that one day PD's story would be told nationally. The *700 Club* Director, Shannon, called before the broadcast to tell us the date and that there was talk of having PD come to Virginia Beach for a live broadcast. I mentioned that there would be a 50 percent chance PD could travel, and in fact, we were not able to join them.

PD and I watched the screening of her testimony on the evening broadcast, not knowing what the final version of the film would be like. As PD and I sat watching together, we were stunned at the beautiful story of her life and how God acted on her behalf. Her testimony of God's grace in her life was broadcast several times in 1990. She never stopped telling people how God healed her of disease and gave her a second chance at life.

# DECISION TO SHARE LIFE TOGETHER AND BE PART OF HER STORY

On December 2, 1977, PD and I were married. Our wedding was in a small chapel at the Orlando Naval Training Center. It had been thirty days since we met. The Navy chaplain wanted to meet with us before the ceremony to get to know us a bit more. He asked if either of us had been married before; PD answered yes, and I answered no. He asked PD if she had children, and she told him of her four sons, her divorce from their father, and custody arrangements. She also explained some of her health history and her current condition. When the chaplain asked me if I had any children, and I answered in the negative, he studied both of us, looked at me, and with a grin stated, "I don't know if I should bless this marriage or order you to psychological counseling!" We all chuckled and agreed that ours was not a normal set of circumstances, but the chaplain concluded the meeting by saying he would be happy to perform the ceremony.

From the time we first met, PD had prayed and asked God to send her someone to love, someone who would love her, and I had prayed and asked God for a wife, just a week or two earlier, as I was about to ship out for duty overseas. I guess I was maturing in thinking that the civilians had gotten it right: a wife, children, a home, and stability. After only our second date, we knew that our petitions to God were answered.

Once PD and I were married, she became a Navy dependent and was allowed access to Orlando's base facilities, including the Navy Exchange and all medical facilities; she would have been well-cared for while I was away at training school in Norfolk, Virginia, and eventually, overseas in Italy.

Leaving our home that morning for training was one of the hardest things I have ever had to do. I called PD every night from Virginia and visited her a few times in Atlanta, where her parents still lived. After finishing six weeks of school and training, our flight departure information was made available, and I took a long walk around the Base and looked at the fleet in the harbor. As I looked at the fleet in port, I thought about leaving the service. I called PD the following evening and discussed my feelings with her; although she did not express it, I could tell she was excited and overjoyed about having me come home to stay. I called the Pentagon and spoke with my detailer, who changed my orders. I never thought I would leave the Navy; it was a difficult decision but one I have never regretted. It was the right thing to do, and although my head said, "Stay," my heart spoke differently. Growing up, I learned to lead with my heart, and I knew this decision was the best for both us and our family.

# PERIOD OF ADJUSTMENT

Adjusting to civilian life, marriage, and becoming a stepfather to little boys was quite a change for me and very challenging. Moreover, PD became extremely ill at the time of my military discharge and required surgery to remove a damaged section of her intestines. Doctors in Orlando were able to help PD somewhat, but she also needed consultations with several surgeons. Finally, a prominent surgeon in Atlanta, one of the best in the nation, agreed to take her case. This new surgeon and his team came to love PD like a daughter as well. We went to Atlanta and stayed with her parents since she had to have many preoperative appointments.

While there, I received a call to return to Orlando for a job interview. The interview was successful, and I was offered the job; it was miraculous how it all happened. I was hired by a large manufacturing firm, which put me on their payroll, with benefits immediately, and used their corporate leverage to return me to Atlanta to be with PD for her surgery. She had suffered so much up to this time, and I could tell she was feeling discouraged. The surgery was performed to repair the damaged intestine. She spent a few weeks in the hospital and stayed with her parents afterward until she was able and strong enough to travel home to Orlando and resume her life.

PD had an inner joy that seemed to radiate and naturally attract people to her. We continued our married life with me working, going to college at night, the boys staying in school, and PD enjoying being a homemaker.

## NEW BEGINNINGS: BUILDING A HOME

We purchased a house in Altamonte Springs and worked to fix it up. She planted a garden and enjoyed caring for it and watching the different vegetables grow. We were amazed and saw every aspect of creativity and His creation. She enjoyed being a mother and was an outstanding example to them—taught them well about truthfulness, helping others in need, friendship, and faithfulness to God above all. She would read stories to them every night and help them with school homework and play with them. There was always a joyful smile, love, and laughter about her, and to this day, her son's greetings always come with a joyful smile and warmth. PD was thrilled to be alive and wanted to give back to God somehow for allowing her a chance at life. She prayed and asked God to show her what she could do to help others come to know Him whose healing hand gave her life when there was no hope for her survival.

PD was interested in real estate; she received her license and worked for Christian Brothers Realty as an associate. She was excellent at this endeavor and was joyful and excited to be working with people to find them the right home to purchase or sell. Most often, after closing, she would give her commission away to the needy or poor with great joy in being able to do so. I would just frown and shake my head and say to myself, "What an amazing person," a selfless gracious lady who always had an attitude of gratitude. After a few years, she gave up real estate work and devoted more time to her children, their schoolwork, and her involvement at church.

From the beginning of our marriage and for many years thereafter, PD experienced stable health. And the medical community marveled because she was not supposed to be alive and doing well. Medically impossible, she was a testament to God's miracle-working power and love for His children.

# THE BRAVE LITTLE SOLDIER WHO JUST WOULDN'T DIE

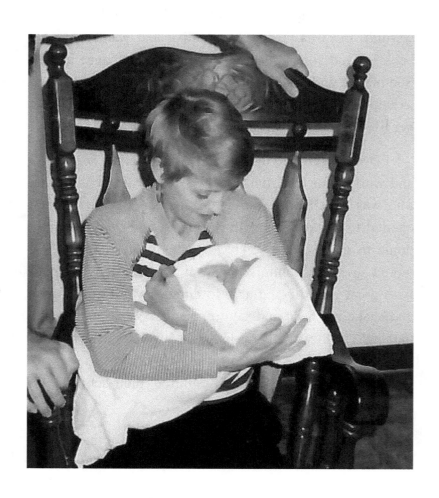

# 4

# IMPOSSIBLE STRUGGLE DESPITE THE ODDS

*PD with first grandchild, Jordan*

We attended a very large church and became involved as Altar Counselors; this was a ministry in which we would talk to those who would come forward at the invitation near the end of every service. This was for those who wanted to receive Jesus as their Lord and Savior or to share with someone about a spiritual issue.

We came to know the other counselors through having shared dinners and fellowship time. We also met before service on Sunday mornings to pray. At one of the evening meetings, after dinner and a sharing of God's Word, the group leader asked if anyone would like to be prayed for. PD looked at me with the widest eyes and said, "I'm going to ask them to pray for me to receive my sight in my blind left eye."

She lost her sight in her left eye while hospitalized for two years, battling to stay alive. Up until this time, she had never asked anyone to pray for God to heal and restore her sight. From the time I first met her and she told me about it, she had always said that one day God was going to restore her sight. There was no question in her mind that it would not be restored. She asked the group to pray for this to happen.

We each laid a hand on her as we gathered around, and a young man prayed a most beautiful prayer over her. When he finished, PD screamed, "I can see! I can see!" Everyone began thanking God; some were crying and overwhelmed; others were stunned at the miracle they just witnessed. PD and I hugged and cried and rejoiced as she always knew by faith that this would happen and never, never doubted for one moment. The living room we were in was fairly dim, so I asked PD to walk across the room and face me. I held up three fingers and asked her how many she saw and on we went, and she got every quiz right from far away and with her right eye covered. Neither of us slept that night, as we were so excited and grateful for God's healing of PD's blind left eye.

## Seeing Through Faith

There was great excitement within the church when they learned what had happened to her. They announced signs and wonders will follow those who believe by faith, to not doubt as PD did about her eyesight. The Word of God says, "Where two or more are gathered in my name, there I will be" and what a moment it was that I will never forget.

The church's senior pastor wanted PD to come to the 6:00 p.m. service that Sunday, and there he told the congregation of the miracle. He introduced PD and told her to share her story about how she lost her eyesight and how it was restored. He then asked her to cover her right eye, to back up, and as he held up his fingers he asked, "How many do you see?" She wore the biggest smile on her face as she named them all, and those in attendance were so thankful to God and praised Him for this healing.

After this, the church became very interested in PD, and questions were asked about her health, and she told how she was healed of Crohn's disease and how she came to know God in a very personal way. So many people wanted to know more about her that I asked her to write a testimony of what God had done in her life.

*"I will praise you to all my brothers; I will stand up before the congregation and testify of the wonderful things you have done"* (Psalm 22:22, TLB). Her doctors stated

that there was no one alive to compare her to—just over three feet of intestines and blood rich in iron, an ongoing miracle.

*"Come and listen, all you who fear God, and I will tell you what he did for me" (Psalm 66:16, NLT).*

# THE LONG ROAD OF SETBACKS

There were many ups and downs with PD's health, including blood chemistry and electrolyte imbalance, which required hospitalization for IV treatments to get her stabilized. Many nights we spent in the emergency room at Orlando Regional Hospital, and always, Dr. Bone would be called to direct her care. It didn't matter to Dr. Bone what time of day it was; he would even come in the middle of the night. To him, PD was his daughter.

On one occasion at the ER, shortly after we married, a nurse was recording PD's information and said, "I used to take care of a person named PD." PD asked, "Was it PD —" and mentioned her last name. The nurse exclaimed, "Yes!" PD smiled and pointed to herself with a big smile. The nurse was thrilled and hugged her and told how the staff talked about PD and thought of her often. The next thing I knew, there were a lot of nurses, including the in-charge nurse, in the room all around her; staff from all over the hospital came to see her as well. The head nurse kissed

PD's head, as did the others. I had backed out of the room, so I stood at the door's entrance and looked on in wonder and amazement at the love and respect they all had for her, as the staff kept coming. It was 2:00 a.m.

On two occasions, PD was hospitalized with double pneumonia and was not expected to live; at one time, a nurse told me to stay close to a phone. After several weeks of care, each time PD would pull through. One hospitalization was for two months, at two different hospitals. She suffered bouts of seizures on several occasions; once I found her in our backyard and had to carry her inside. There were sudden hospital emergency room trips many times as her face and jaw would lock up because of a lack of potassium in her blood or from a total electrolyte imbalance. IV solutions were administered, and she would not be released until her blood results were stable.

PD's doctors decided that a permanent IV access port should be installed in her chest for administering medicine and withdrawing blood. It was decided she would be on home health care after this procedure.

Tubing was installed in her chest with an access port hooked up to a solution bag, which was shipped to our home weekly. A home health care nurse would come by once per week to check on PD's vitals and to draw blood. The lab results would then be given to the pharmacist and her primary care physician. The nurse would also change the chest needle under aseptic conditions, and I would administer the IVs each night: four each week, for four hours each time.

The pharmacist would copy her lab results and pre-mix the IV solutions accordingly. The pharmacist called her every Tuesday morning and PD would let her know what other supplies she needed, and they would be delivered that week. With the home health care nurses, doctors, and pharmacists all working together as a team, her blood chemistry was kept in check.

> *"I want you all to know about the miraculous signs and wonders the Highest God has performed for me" (Daniel 4:2, NLT).*

## THE TORTUROUS REHAB

There were many, many trips to the hospitals for various reasons as the years went by. For about two years, she suffered from terrible, debilitating migraines: only an injection of a strong narcotic would be able to break the pain. Doctors had no answers on how to treat these migraines, so she suffered until, finally, after much prayer, the migraine pains suddenly stopped. God answered.

Middle-of-the-night emergency room runs were common and over the years, she was hospitalized for months, dealing with electrolyte imbalances, seizures, migraines, pneumonia, and other conditions. Both of her hands contracted staph infections and were almost amputated at one point. Each day, her hands were unwrapped and underwent surgery until all of the infection was diminished. There was no skin or flesh left on either hand, only tendons and bone.

After four days, the surgeon told me he was able to save her hands, but she would barely be able to use them, as the damage was so extensive. He said he had never seen anything that bad. Both of her hands were completely bandaged, and an IV pump was set up with morphine for pain. I had a family member next to her bed around the clock each day. For over two excruciating months, she couldn't do anything for herself.

I was with her the first time a nurse took her bandages off and placed both hands in a whirlpool bath with a salt solution. A scrub brush was used to clean off the bacteria that was forming around the outer edges of her skin. Before starting the treatment, she was given additional pain medicine that was to the limit she could have without killing her. It was very painful for her.

I was in there; she didn't cry out as the nurse placed her hands into the bath; she stared straight ahead, but the side of her face was quivering.

I almost passed out when I saw her hands and had to leave the room for a while. This went on each day as the new flesh and skin were forming. She was also placed in a hyperbaric chamber each day for a specified time with a nurse by her side as this method was used to enhance the healing time for both hands.

Many weeks went by in the hospital while her hands were healing. Then came rehabilitation for three weeks at another section of the hospital to teach her how to dress, care for her ostomy, and care for herself. Although she had her hands, she had lost up to 90 percent of use on each hand. On each hand, only the thumb and right and left index fingers worked; the other three would not work and had no movement. Not only did she have limited use of her hands, but the negative psychological impact on her was very serious and overwhelming to the point she felt her life was over and often wished she would die.

# A Homecoming: But Little Good News

Upon bringing her home, I had arranged for her sister, Tracy, to live with us and assist. PD eventually learned how to dress and care for her personal needs. Being able to empty her ostomy pouch and change it when needed was a huge hurdle for her to overcome. She was able to put on her makeup but needed help washing her hair at times. Cooking took her most of the day, but she was determined to provide a wonderful meal for me each evening and always looked her best and greeted me with the biggest smile and hug each night when I came home from work.

At this time, the business of home health care was coming into its own, where seasoned, highly qualified nurses would regularly visit patients assigned to them at the patients' homes. The blood lab results would be faxed to her doctor and pharmacists and medicine added to the IV bag. Because her veins were so tiny and weak and often collapsed, it was often difficult getting an IV needle into a vein, so permanent IV tubing and a port were recommended for her to have. I remember the afternoon that I was in the hospital room for pre-op, and PD's surgeon came in to visit. He explained what would be taking place in the morning, and also that she was a risk because of her history.

## GOD HONORED ME TO HELP HER COPE

While she was napping, I started to feel very down about it all and sorry for her and myself. As the sun was starting to set, I found I had a Navy league magazine with me that was given to me by the plant manager at the factory where I worked. He knew I was a Navy vet with many years of service. I sat next to the window and used the sun for light.

The room lights were turned off, and I opened the magazine to the middle, where there was the beginning of a story by a Marine who served in Vietnam and was stationed at Kheshan. He told of this historic battle where every third or fourth Marine was either killed or wounded. Tears filled my eyes as I looked at the picture of the few survivors and thought of what they went through. These men were my age and gave their lives, and I was living.

I closed the magazine and said to myself, "I have no problem," as I had a chance at a life when so many my age never had, and I think about that often. I thanked God for showing me and never felt sorry for myself again. During all my time in the Navy, I was trained to embrace discomfort and rigorous and impossible situations. However, nothing could have prepared me for the war that would have been awaiting me at home with my wife and her illness. One learns to respect men who have it hard, choose to go through it, and overcome, and I know the men I served with would have been proud of PD.

# The Heartbreak of Dialysis

At this point, PD was at risk when going into virtually every operation. Once again, we were told, "She might not make it." Each time before wheeling her in, the surgeon and the anesthesiologist would visit PD beforehand and, with an endearing smile, pat her lovingly. They knew her medical history and had tremendous respect for what she had gone through. More than one doctor told me that doctors never quite met anyone like her, and the nurses would all be pulling for her. Each time before taking her to the operating room, they would let me have a few minutes alone for us to tell of our love for each other and that she would be waiting for me if she didn't come through. These were very precious moments.

PD was on dialysis at this point, for her kidneys had failed to clean up the toxins in her blood to an acceptable level and, therefore, she needed the dialysis process. An operation was performed to install large tubing under her skin, with one end connected to an artery and the other to a vein. Her blood was pumped out of her artery through a filtration system and back into the veins. Needles were inserted into the artery and vein side each time she received the treatment.

She got to know everyone at the dialysis center: nurses, doctors, and technicians, and they loved taking care of her and would assign only the best technicians to watch over her. PD would often ask the other patients their names, and I noticed that they would all smile whenever they saw her. She was the only one that I saw over her years going to the treatment center that was ever consistently treated that way with the love and respect they all had for her. They somehow knew that she was different and special; it was the love of God within her. Dr. Warren, a well-respected nephrologist, once told me that he had never met anyone quite like her. He was amazed at her medical history and always showed great respect for her.

## INCREDIBLE GRACE UNDER WITHERING FIRE

Going to and through the dialysis process was a dreadful struggle for PD. The preparation before leaving the house was a challenge, as PD never left home without looking her best. However, it took time for her to get ready with only limited use of her hands. Even when she wasn't feeling well, she would always smile and become so loving toward other patients and staff. She would get to know all of them and would make cookies for certain ones, encouraging them with words and thoughts.

I would always have a nurse, experienced caregiver, or a family member help her get ready and take her to treatments. They would stay and bring her home when the treatment was completed. I normally would take her at least one day each week. She would be exhausted afterward, as all the treated patients were. With all the hospitalizations and operations, thirty-five at that point, with all IVs, blood draws, wound dressings, and such, during painful treatments in all the years I had known her, she never once complained or became angry.

Several times, I would have to leave the hospital room in tears. It was no wonder the nurses wanted her for their patient, as more than one would tell me she smiles through the pain and tells them it's all right; it was no wonder that nurses would come to visit her at our house and drive from other cities, such as Jacksonville, as they would hear of some serious condition and would find out when PD would be released from a hospital and wanted to see her and how she was doing.

It was also no wonder what I witnessed at two a.m. in the emergency room of Orlando Regional Medical Center when the word got out that PD was to be there on a visit. Nurses, head nurses, housekeepers, and other staff came to see her and love on her and kiss her head; it was an amazing and unbelievable sight. Her key doctor, gastroenterologist Frank Bone, who always appeared up and dressed at those late hours, once told me that he was there to give special instructions to the team because PD was "his girl." All her doctors showed unusual respect and admiration for PD. She was so brave and strong, and more than once, I had doctors tell me that they had never met anyone quite like her.

Off-duty nurses also would come to visit because they loved, respected, and admired her, and they would always receive more of God's blessing than they gave in coming to see her. To them, she was what nursing was all about. PD was not a whiner or complainer, but was dealt a tough hand in life and played it well.

# 5

# HER GREATEST TREASURE: GREATEST LOSS

*Brandon, Derek, PD, Jared, and Theron*

As mentioned earlier, PD had four sons: Theron, Derek, Jared, and Brandon; less than two years apart, they were very close as babies and children and remain close to this day. PD was with her babies and nurtured each with the love, affection, and joy that can only come from a mother. She saw it as a special gift from God and was so thankful to God for them. They were with her as she would read children's stories to them with joy and laughter. You see her influence in each of their lives today, and it's so very evident as each has a love for reading, a love of laughter, and joy, just like their mother.

*"Train up a child in the way he should go, and when he is old he will not depart from it"* *(Proverbs 22:6, KJV).*

# TRAIN UP A CHILD IN THE WAY HE SHOULD GO

Every day since the birth of her children, PD prayed earnestly for them to become good men who would have godly wives and children who would become good citizens. She prayed in earnest for each to know Jesus Christ as their Lord and Savior and that she would be with them in Heaven for all Eternity without end. She was overjoyed to know that the two oldest did accept Jesus into their hearts and are living out their lives for Him each day. PD was burdened for them, especially as she was unable to raise them because of the divorce and their move to Montana, where they were raised by their father. She was faithful in prayer for them and holding onto God's promise.

She saw God's answer firsthand when her oldest son told her the good news the night before his wedding in Montana. As he walked her to our car, he privately told her he had prayed a prayer with Judy's pastor. Judy was raised in the church and was a strong and committed Christian girl. Judy was the answer to PD's prayers of many years, and she was beaming at their wedding and so thankful to God. Today, after more than thirty years of marriage and raising four beautiful, successful children, she was so grateful to God to be able to live long enough to see them grow and become good young women and men.

## THE GLORY OF MOTHERHOOD, DESPITE THE CHALLENGES

PD made an album for each one of her sons with pictures of them when they were babies growing up. She wrote beautiful letters to them about their birth and being babies and expressed her deepest love as only a mother could. It was as if she felt she might not be around to personally tell them of their birth, baby years, and early childhood. She wanted them to know and have the album to remember her by and again to express to each one with her beautiful gift of writing her love. She marveled and thanked God for each one.

I looked at the one album and read the letter she wrote to Theron, her first. I cried most of the weekend. I realized how beautiful it was, and I know Theron will treasure this and the photo album for his entire life. He has a beautiful heritage with his brothers, each unique and different from one another, whose memories of their mother will never cease, and their mom's love for each will remain with them throughout their lives.

# Theron

Each son was so special to PD in his own way. Theron, the firstborn, was adored by his mom and was carefully and lovingly raised. He was also the first grandchild of each set of grandparents and was so loved. Theron loved to draw and was very talented. From early childhood, it was evident that he was gifted at imagining something and being able to put it on paper in an expressive way. He continued drawing through his high school years. Two of his beautiful paintings that were done in his high school years hang in our home today.

While Theron was in high school, he told his mother that after graduation, he was thinking of going to Hollywood to study art. At this, PD became very concerned as her comments to me were that if he were to go there; she may never see him again. She prayed fervently about this and often as she was troubled by Theron's plan.

Within a few months, her prayers were answered. After getting ready for church on a Sunday morning, I picked up our newspaper, and the headlines read, "Disney World to Build MGM Studios at Disney." I smiled and felt peace and joy about it, wondering, "What if…?" PD was still getting ready, and I said nothing about this but placed the paper in our den where I knew she would see the headline. I was in the back of the house, and I heard PD shout out, "Thank You, Jesus! Hallelujah! Thank You, Lord! Kevin! Kevin! Disney is going to build MGM Studios for Theron to come to work here and not Hollywood. God answered my prayer, Kev." She was so excited. She kept thanking God and was so happy about it.

There was no question in her mind about the news. This was God's answer to her prayers for Theron. She knew it. I can just imagine God smiling at PD's reaction. She couldn't wait until that night, so she could call Theron to tell him God was building MGM Studios for him at Disney. She sent him the announcement, and I didn't know it, but she wrote on it. All this took place several years before the construction of MGM began, and PD never doubted.

Theron and his wife, Judy, eventually came to Orlando, Florida, where he worked at a few places. Then one night his mother and I chose to babysit their children, as they had a date night. When they came back, I asked how his job was doing, and he told me he was working for Disney. I asked, "Doing what?"

His eyes moistened, and he humbly told me, "The Art Director for Disney MGM Studios." I was stunned, and he had tears in his eyes. I asked him if he remembered the phone call from his mother and the article from the paper's announcement. He said he still had the article. I asked him if Mom had written on it. "Yes, she did," he answered. I told him to forever keep that article to pass on to his children and grandchildren as a testimony of faith in God to believe that He would answer the prayers of a mother's troubled heart. When we told his mom about his job at Disney, she just smiled and congratulated him, as she knew from the time of the announcement that this was an answer to her prayers for Theron

Today, after more than twenty years of a successful career at Disney, he is a former Imagineering Creative Vice President of the Disney Cruise Lines, and there was never any doubt in PD's mind that God had Disney build MGM Studios at Walt Disney World for Theron. Never! Theron married Judy, who is a precious and wonderful wife, mother, and a faithful woman of God. Judy was raised in the church from day one by faith-filled parents; she meets the definition of a "Proverbs 31 woman."

PD loved each of her grandchildren and cherished the little time she spent with each. She loved seeing them grow and hearing of their accomplishments. The oldest of her grandchildren, Jordan, is an advanced nurse practitioner. Both grandsons, Logan and Collin, are combat veterans, one in the Marines and the other in the Air Force, Special Forces. The youngest, Megan, recently graduated from college. Growing up, they lived in Paris, France for over two years and in Hong Kong, Asia for four years. Additionally, the family has visited over thirty-five countries collectively. PD was very proud and truly loved each one.

# DEREK

Derek, PD's second oldest son, married Ronalee (Roni).

Roni was the second expectant mother to come to PD when she was ministering to girls during pregnancy out of wedlock. PD told me after her first meeting with Roni that she was different from other unwed mothers, as Roni was very poised, intelligent, well-spoken, attractive, and had a charming personality. PD thought of Roni as an Ivy League, private girls' school student. PD loved Roni very much and always was joyful and appreciative of her, staying so close to her as the years went by. Roni would simply drop by for an informal visit with PD, take her shopping, set her hair, help her cook, and just spend some quality time with her.

A few times Roni's youngest son, Tyler, spent time at our house and got to know PD, and she loved every minute of being with him. She would tell me how sweet and precious he was. Today, Tyler is serving in the Air Force. He and his wife named their daughter after PD.

After her first marriage failed, Derek eventually married Roni. Derek and Roni live in Montana, where he is termed out, Montana State Legislature for his district, and from what I'm told, is a sought-after speaker at political rallies and supporter of other candidates. He is a Conservative and Constitutionalist and is gifted at policy making and debating. Derek is known as a trusted ally for well-known politicians and has his finger on the pulse of Montana politics.

Derek kept in close contact with his mother, asking her to pray for him at times. She was always thrilled to hear from him and loved both of them very much. She was very touched to hear there were one hundred men who met weekly at a large church in Montana on Friday mornings to pray and have fellowship. These men were ranchers, and together they would pray for PD. She was really moved by this. As I write this, I was informed that Derek won his reelection, taking seventy-one percent of the vote in his district and was elected Majority Whip by his peers within the State Legislature. His mother would say, "That's my boy." I believe that from Heaven, she is aware of all this and very proud of him as she was with all her sons, no matter what.

# JARED

Jared was PD's third son. PD told me that as a baby and young child, he always wanted to be with his mother. He wouldn't let anyone else hold him and would always cling to her. He just felt better being next to his mom. Psychology teaches that the formation of a child's understanding of the world at large is established between one and five years, and statistics support the fact that when one of the child's parents is missing during those years, it is most likely to have adverse consequences. PD was hospitalized for more than two years during Jared's formative phase, and this no doubt had an effect on him. PD felt that if any of her sons were affected by her being gone so long, it would have been Jared.

He became a thoughtful, kind, and loving person who was an excellent builder and trim carpenter. While living in Montana, he met and married Michelle, whom PD loved from their first meeting. When Jared moved to Florida, he visited his mother often; they had a close relationship.

We hired Jared to do many odd jobs around the house. I noticed that when he put on his tool belt, it was like a total paradigm shift took place in him. He was down to business to complete the task at hand. The work Jared did was second to none in any trade. Jared was also highly skilled and very intelligent. He was hard-working and maintained a cheerful attitude like his mom. I was not surprised when Walt Disney World hired him to work with their project team, supervising the contracted firms that performed various, often large, construction-like projects for Disney.

Jared often worked the midnight shift, as that's when a large portion of the park's projects would commence. I would call and talk with him a few times in the early morning hours and always enjoyed listening to him, as he seemed to be positive, upbeat, and always cheerful. One time I called him at 4:00 a.m.; it was freezing cold outside. He was stationed at Hollywood Studios, and he had contractors working in the cold doing a large project. He was in the process of making hot chocolate for them and would take it to them in a large thermos to help warm them up. This he did often, as he knew from experience how hard it was to have to work outside at that temperature. He had great compassion for these non-native laborers, once telling me about the look they would give him when he did this; it was a look of gratefulness, respect, and love that a company representative would do something so kind and thoughtful for them as they were often overlooked as just laborers.

No one told Jared to do this, but his heart did, and this was telling of the kind of man he had become. His mom was so proud of him. PD would always say of him and her other sons when we would hear about a kind or generous act they would do for total strangers, "That's my boy."

Jared married Michelle, a girl who grew up in Montana and was raised by a single mother. They had no children, and tragically, Jared's life ended as the result of a terrible automobile accident after leaving his shift one morning and heading home.

His death was a staggering blow to PD. Only God could ease the pain. PD mourned for months afterward, crying herself to sleep each night and often bursting into tears when people would ask how many sons she had. For a woman of strong faith, who trusted God for strength to make it through the day, her loss of Jared was unspeakable. Having already suffered pain like few others, she now faced what many have described as life's most painful—the loss of a child.

Several years after his death, PD said that she wouldn't want Jared to come back after his being in Heaven all this time. Jared was a believing Christian man, not perfect, but he honored God, and today is reunited with his mother in Heaven for eternity.

# BRANDON

The youngest of PD's four sons is Brandon. Many times, his mother would tell me how close she had come to losing him during her pregnancy and how thankful to God she was that he was born. What a loss it would have been for both of them.

Brandon was just two and a half years old when his mother was hospitalized for over two years, fighting to stay alive. Brandon didn't recognize his mom when she came home. PD always felt that Brandon was greatly affected by their separation.

As mentioned, PD was given custody of Jared and Brandon after being back home for only a few months. PD only wanted the best for her sons whom she so loved, and it hurt her heart deeply as she gave up custody of her older two sons. She was left with the two youngest, as she knew she was too sickly to raise all four boys properly. Given a split family, there was often a serious amount of pressure to stay with his older brothers in beautiful Montana when visiting during the summer vacations. Jared stayed one year and didn't return. Brandon always returned, coming back to his mom, with no brothers, only him to be with his mom.

PD poured herself into raising Brandon. She read to him every night, dropped him off and picked him up from school, and would help him with homework. Neighbors would ask if they could hire Brandon to do some chores for them, especially for this older disabled lady across the street from us. PD taught Brandon not to take money from the elderly—especially Mrs. B., as she was known as this woman who lived alone and was wheelchair bound. She always needed some help. Brandon would do this willingly and cheerfully. He loved to help others in need, giving of himself to others, and expecting nothing in return. I am proud to say this character virtue has been most evident from Brandon's childhood and throughout his life. He learned this from his mom as he witnessed the practically non-stop giving of his mom to the young women who came to her for help while being in a crisis pregnancy. He shared his life with many of the girls who stayed with us, especially Rachel, who loved Brandon as the little brother she never had.

Throughout the years, there were so many hospitalizations, during which PD sometimes teetered near death, but Brandon was there each time with me. I would pull him out of school and go to the hospital, and all through his adult years, he was there for her each and every time. His mom often remarked to me, "Just think, Kev, I almost lost him." Brandon would always do things for his mom without being asked. She cherished his beautiful writings on the most amazing beautiful Mother's Day cards, which she read over and over; she kept every one of them. Year in and year out, Brandon came to dinner every Thursday night, regardless of how he felt (I could often tell when he had a rough day), but he would come regardless, for he knew how his mom so looked forward to seeing him.

I would wake PD before leaving for work each morning and give her pain medication and help her to the bathroom. She always woke with the biggest smile when learning it was Thursday and was excited that she would see Brandon that evening for dinner. It was extra special for her. Brandon's wife knew early on that Thursday night was dinner at his mom's house.

Amy's mother commented to me once that when Amy first told her about this, she said that she knew then that Brandon was special. Special indeed; over the years, he was always there for her, whether middle-of-the-night hospital trips, weekends by her bedside, repairs around the homestead, or seeing a need and filling it.

Brandon never had to be asked; rather, he did it out of love, honor, and respect for his mom. He witnessed firsthand the love a godly woman had for the lost, lonely, downtrodden, forgotten, and hurting people of this world. The love she had and care for her animals, the uncommon, became common in Brandon's life. The above was just a snapshot of his life and many stories could be told of what he experienced growing up and the precious memories that he has of PD, which without question, I know he will cherish forever.

## The Amazing Case of Ronalee "Roni"

As I mentioned earlier, Derek's wife, Ronalee's case was quite unusual. She joined PD's world and family first by spiritual need, then in mutual love of the Lord, and finally by actual marriage. She describes her spiritual adventure with PD in her own words.

"Imagine standing on the edge of a shimmering lake. You pick up a stone to skim it across the water. As soon as the stone touches the surface of the water, a ripple forms that becomes larger and larger. The ripple effect is so much greater than the original impact formed by a single stone.

"I am fascinated by the theory that the flutter of a butterfly's wings can cause a hurricane on the other side of the world. If you change the smallest of life's details, you completely change its outside. A single occurrence, no matter how small, can change the course of nature forever.

"I have recently been thinking about my dear mother-in-law PD and all that she has come to mean to our family. She was so deeply dedicated to each of us. I think too about all the abandoned girls who, because of GOD's love, are no longer lost but are now leading joyful lives. PD did not stay on her knees, tucked away in prayer. She lived her faith and honored a call in her life to minister to young girls and women who were in crisis. She became a force of nature that changed many lives forever.

"All of us can tell the story of PD's grace and endurance through the unimaginable pain that was the illness we saw in her physical suffering. To know PD was to know that she was so much more than that. She was grace, oh yes, grace.

"A mighty warrior in life—and in her fierce faith that would lead her, guide her, and comfort her. That faith and knowledge, not belief, but that confidence in really knowing deep inside. She knew that God had given her the heart to be an advocate to reach the lost, unlovable, and hurting girls who lived unseen among us.

"I know this passion personally. I met PD twenty-nine years ago, one of those hurting girls—eighteen, pregnant, homeless, and uncertain about what my future was going to be. You see, I had no worth, no value, and saw myself as little more than garbage to be used and discarded.

"That was what my experience had been up to that time. I was a girl who was in a world that physically, emotionally, and sexually abused me from the time I was ten years old. And this woman looked me in the eyes and said to me, "You are a beautiful and remarkable person." She told me, "God has etched you on my heart and He has a plan for you. A plan that is good; for hope and not despair."

"She gave me a chance for hope. She found me a home with a family who served as volunteers in the ministry and committed to getting girls off the streets. My son was born shortly after that day. She was there with me, and she never left me or abandoned me since. PD taught me life lessons and always loved everyone unconditionally. She did not judge me or try to force her faith and values—she lived them. Not just for me, but for over eighty girls like me.

"I made a life decision that took me on a journey, but I was somehow always anchored in PD's love. It took me a while, but her patience and prayers won in the end. You see, I was fortunate to have had the wings of PD brush up against the story of my life, and that forever altered the course of nature. But her legacy has many ripples and continues to change the course of nature, as with this girl whom she chose to make her daughter, who became her daughter-in-law, and who has given the beautiful gift of a great-granddaughter, Patricia, born just over three weeks ago. Patricia is a beautiful tiny bundle of tenaciousness like her namesake and will know the story of how one woman's commitment to be in ministry, even when she herself should have been the one ministered to, changed lives. Remember the ripples—thousands of them from one small pebble.

"I remember so vividly, that PD prayed for her sons, prayers that included a desire for them to marry loving and godly wives. PD stepped out in faith and ministries to a broken girl and changed her life forever- who became that godly woman.

"I loved PD and I am glad that she was able to see in her life how she changed the course of my life forever. Today I know that from her new vantage point, God's view, she will see those thousands of ripples that have forever changed the nature of many generations. One small pebble who listened to the call of ministry, and through great perseverance brought hope out of despair."

—Ronalee "Roni" Skees

# 6

# OPENING HER HEART AND HER HOME: PD'S MINISTRY OF LOVE

*PD in her home, Florida*

Despite all the medical afflictions and daily sufferings that commanded most of PD's daily affairs for years, she came to realize, with the intensity of the warrior she was, that God would no longer bless America as long as it continued to condone the murder of our children in the womb. So

THE BRAVE LITTLE SOLDIER WHO JUST WOULDN'T DIE

she did something. Turning her attention to the sheltering of young women who were pregnant out of wedlock, PD ultimately became a major force in Central Florida against institutionalized abortion. Results of her efforts have taken on new vigor today with the growing emphasis on pro-life support organizations PD had a hand in founding. In the early 1980s, PD became horrified to learn about the abortions happening in the nation. She prayed and prayed to God about it, and His answer came for her to do something about it. Her exact prayer was, "God, please do something to stop the killing of these precious little babies." She asked what she was to do, as she had no money or enough influence, and no one seemed to care. His answer came to her, and it was to shepherd homes for these girls who were often told by parents, husbands, and boyfriends when they found out about the pregnancy to either get an abortion or get out.

PD talked to me about this burden placed on her by God one night, and she had a look in her eyes I hadn't seen before. I had this strong feeling not to push back about her burden, and little did I know that a spark was lit that would ignite into a blaze throughout Florida and beyond. For weeks, PD made phone calls to different churches and ministries throughout the country, finding out what others were doing about abortion in their states and communities. Most of the ministries sent her information about their programs. A lady named Barbara, who was local, was the director of the only known pregnancy center that provided examinations and counseling to the girls who went or were sent there due to an unwanted pregnancy. Barbara was a very good resource for PD and, of course, they became close friends.

PD spent countless hours calling and seeking answers. Thomas Roads First Baptist Church in Virginia was also very helpful in providing information. She became so well known that the Reverend Jerry Falwell's secretary called and invited us to breakfast with him when he was visiting Orlando once. PD was on fire and worked tirelessly, gathering information and listening to what other ministries and churches were doing throughout the nation.

There was very little to no support for the girls, other than to listen to a sidewalk counselor who was picketing out front of the abortion clinics. These faithful souls would call out to a young girl entering the abortion clinic, and some of the girls would come and talk with them. Once they saw photos of what their baby was like and explained that it was more than just a blob, the girls, for the most part, were horrified at the thought of killing it as these photos showed the baby's actual formation for their month of pregnancy. Inside the clinics, the abortion clinics did not show any of this to these young girls.

It often frightened and confused them with little to no other choice but to abort the pregnancy. Once convinced that it was the wrong thing to do, the next question would be, "Where do I go?" "What can I do?" At this, the counselors had no answer, and that's when PD stepped up after getting a phone call from a sidewalk counselor whom she did not know, but who had heard about her.

## Saving Rachel

PD was told that a young nineteen-year-old girl was on her way into the abortion clinic when a sidewalk counselor called out to her, and they talked. This person asked if she and our family would be willing to take her into our home, as the young man she lived with told her to get an abortion or get out. She had no other place to go. PD told me about this, and once again with that certain look of conviction, she said, "Kev, if we take her in, you'll see things happen against abortion all over this city." PD then told me that this girl was nineteen, from Pennsylvania, had an abortion at age sixteen, was arrested and jailed for drug possession, lived with the town's drug dealer, and was arrested and jailed for attempted manslaughter. She ran away with this guy who was with a traveling circus. There was no introduction; sight unseen, we both agreed to take her in.

Her name was Rachel, and she had a lot of wild rough edges, to say the least. We gave her one of our spare bedrooms and treated her as one of the family. It was awkward at first, but it wasn't long before we settled in and felt comfortable with one another. PD would have long talks with her each night, counseling, guiding her, encouraging, and inspiring her. PD worked hard to set up Rachel's medical care through government agencies. Dental and medical treatments were provided by volunteer doctors and dentists. PD bought her maternity clothes and necessities.

Now and then, Rachel would leave and go back to the apartment where her boyfriend was to take care of the dog. PD and I became suspicious of this but said nothing and trusted God. A few weeks went by, and I read a story in the daily newspaper, the Orlando Sentinel, about two people who were killed while cave diving at DeLeon Springs. One of the two who drowned was Rachel's boyfriend, the one she ran away with. Instinctively, I sensed the seriousness of the event and God's hand in this. Rachel was stunned and in shock as the father of her child was now deceased. We never talked about his death, only that all people who ever lived have a date with destiny.

From that moment on, Rachel began to change and started going to church with us; we could tell she hadn't been to church in quite a while. We quickly introduced her to other girls in her age group, and they took her to church with them on Thursday nights at a young adult ministry at the church.

Rachel was introduced, and the group all immediately accepted and loved her. She told PD that she didn't feel ashamed or embarrassed about being a soon-to-be single mother out of wedlock; they all extended the love of God to her.

# A Struggle with the Spirits of Abortion

I would call PD every day at noon to see how she was, and one time she told me that Rachel was rebellious and rude to her and that she had thoughts of asking her to leave. At dinner that evening, PD and I talked, and she mentioned that this came on all of a sudden, and she didn't understand. We paused, and the thought came to me that Rachel's rebellious spirit was out of Hell and not God. Instantly, we both realized that this work might fail with her. We both prayed together for her that night before bed and put the outcome in God's hands, trusting Him.

I woke up very early the next morning for some reason and couldn't get back to sleep. There was a powerful presence that I hadn't felt ever before, and I knew the presence was evil. I got up and rebuked this devil or demon and in my spirit was rebuking this presence from one room to the next, so that he or they would not cause Rachel to fail, and this baby would be born. I was in a rage. "You won't have her! Get out of this house, in the name of Jesus!"

I kept it up through each room and finally, I opened the front door and gestured by grabbing and throwing the presence out and went down our driveway pointing my finger at this evil spirit yelling, "You never come back, in the name of Jesus!"

I then went and grabbed a bottle of oil and knelt at each

door in the house, placed my hand on each and prayed for God's protection, and anointed each door casing with the oil.

It was around 4:30 a.m. when this happened. If a neighbor walking outside saw me throwing and pointing my finger at nothing with anger down our driveway, surely the police would have been called. No one in the house was up and had no idea of what had taken place early that morning.

I made my usual call at noon that day and PD told me she did not know what had happened, but Rachel was being so sweet and kind, like her old self. She was amazed. I thanked God and learned a powerful lesson from the experience. "Greater is He that is in me, God, than he that is in the world" and there is the ultimate authority in the name of Jesus.

I shared with PD that night what took place early that morning and she was thrilled. We had finally recognized where this sudden change in Rachel's behavior had come from. If we had failed and given up on her, there probably wouldn't have been the eighty-seven other girls that followed behind her in this anti-abortion ministry. This ministry developed into possibly hundreds of other ministries that would have been delayed if PD had given up.

Several crisis pregnancy centers came to life on PD's watch. These ministries have developed into significant ministries, having a hand in preventing the murder of thousands of babies within the Orlando and Central Florida community. PD had become the informal Pro-Life leader in the Orlando area, and one of the national leaders said to us that what was happening in Orlando was the model for the nation. PD received invitations to speak and attend building dedications, fundraising events, banquets, marches for life, and press conferences. She would politely decline all invitations to speak for herself because she was concerned about all the attention she was receiving, taking pride in the accomplishments and progress made. Only once did PD attend a large press conference, for the Right-to-Life anniversary held in a large ballroom at a Holiday Inn.

The churches begged her to come—she didn't know that she was to be placed on the podium and asked to speak to the gathering of reporters and TV news present. She had no notes or any preparation for what might be asked, but she had God in her heart and the Holy Spirit. She spoke to them so beautifully and eloquently about the programs, different ministries, the girls, and the changes in their lives, and how God was moving in their lives. She spoke with passion and with humility, love, and joy. God was present; the press probably sensed something was different, as when she was finished, not one question was asked of her. I believe God spoke through her, and all present knew it.

# Love Makes the Difference

Several months went by, and Rachel started reaching out to her sisters back in her hometown and surrounding area. She would always end the call by saying, "I love you" to them. This was a first for them, as their family was not raised, or used to, hearing that they were loved by one another. During conversations with her, they began to realize their sister had gone through a change for the better and were amazed. Shortly thereafter, one of the sisters came down to see her. Immediately upon meeting Rachel, the sister burst into tears of gratitude; she was so grateful to see the change in Rachel. Not long after this, Rachel's father came and was so humbled and thankful, and PD, never being one to want praise, deflected all thanksgiving and praise to God, and she repeatedly reminded all that she was just a servant doing the Lord's work.

Months went by, and Rachel started going to church with PD and me. On Sunday mornings, the members saw she was pregnant and due at any time, and they loved her, not knowing anything about her story. They just saw that Rachel was an unwed mother who was alone and trusting and believing in God. The day finally came when I was called to leave work, and I raced to the hospital. PD was in the delivery room with Rachel, and I was outside the room with her friend, Beth, on our knees listening at the bottom of the double doors for any sounds of birth.

Finally, after much bustling around inside, came some familiar utterances of a precious newborn baby crying, and our hearts melted with gratitude and joy to God for the life of this precious one that may not have been.

PD taught Rachel about motherhood for her baby, and how beautiful it was to see her grow and mature into womanhood. The baby's name was David; he was such a good infant. A local TV channel heard about Rachel's story and interviewed her, PD, and me. The interview was recorded on a TV channel, and the host was very gracious to us. With cameras rolling, it started, and we all had a piece to say about what it was like to have Rachel with us. PD talked about how proud she was of Rachel and with her decision to keep and raise her baby. When Rachel told her story, she was nervous but told it beautifully and ended with bursting into tears and burying her face in her hands, and PD reached out to hold her in her arms. This was a powerful, touching moment. The studio cameramen, lighting technician, and hostess all were visibly touched. The director and others were in tears.

Rachel's last sentence was, "If it weren't for PD, I don't know what I would have done." Then, all the emotions poured forth. The film went to our church at that time and was shown at all services. Many people within the church wanted to know more and wanted to help.

# Beginning a Rededication to Life

A few months went by, and a baby dedication service was going to be held at an evening service at Calvary Church where Rachel's baby would be prayed for by the church's pastor. The church was filled that night as people came from all over Central Florida and even Lakewood for the special occasion and service, as they had heard Rachel's story.

PD, Rachel, and I sat on the front row that was reserved for us, and the service started. The pastor gave a sermon that led to Rachel and her decision to keep her baby. The pastor mentioned the many Pro-Life leaders from different denominations that were there and recognized each one. It was a beautiful opening to what was an amazing service.

The moment came for us to go up to the altar. Cameras were going in the back. The church had called earlier in the day and asked PD if, after the baby was dedicated, she would speak about the girls and the Pro-Life ministry with the girls. I asked her if she had written any notes or anything to talk from, and she very calmly said that she prayed and was going to let God speak through her.

I was nervous for her, as there were hundreds of people there; she stepped up to the microphone and spoke about how God had given her a burden to do something about abortion. She spoke about her journey with Rachel and what it meant to be able to serve God in this way. She spoke for several minutes, eloquently and beautifully. I knew it was God speaking through her, and by the look on the pastors' faces, they also knew.

# CENTER IS BORN: UNDER PD'S QUIET LEADERSHIP

PD was a well-spoken lady and very intelligent. At one point specifically, she said with passion and humility that "in the heart of all these girls is a treasure and we just have to help them find it." A few sentences later, she ended her remarks and looked at Rachel and told her how much she loved her, and that she was the best thing that ever happened to her. At that, the whole church rose to its feet and clapped loudly and long along with some shouts. The service ended with a prayer of thanksgiving.

People were lined up to meet PD, many crying and asking what they could do to help her cause. People of all professions—doctors, dentists, lawyers—all quietly offered to help, with no charges. It was a special night, and many, if not all the leaders of other churches, wanted to meet her as well. That night, an older wealthy gentleman who was at the service must have been touched, as the next day he met with the pastor and gave several million dollars to help these girls and the abortion ministry. He wanted a home for the girls with a full-time director paid for with the interest from the money. The church established a board with PD as its leader.

PD and I were invited to a Life Group meeting, and she was asked if she would speak about the girls and the ministry. We were seated for dinner, and PD was seated next to the older gentleman that had been so generous in giving. He was a precious man and, upon leaving, patted PD's hand and assured her that more money would be coming to fund this ministry.

## THE BEGINNINGS OF A LEGACY FOR LIFE

A building was purchased along busy I-4 highway, between Fairbanks and Lee Road, and a crisis pregnancy center was established there. Girls could come there and have free pregnancy tests and also counseling on motherhood, adoption if they chose, medical, etc. The staff were all licensed counselors with postgraduate degrees in these particular areas of need. The ministry was launched, and the date was set for the dedication of the building, which was formerly known as "Life for Kids." Many phone calls were made to PD, and specially written invitations asked her to attend the building dedication ceremony, as it was her vision and love for these girls that touched the hearts of so many.

## PD: "ONLY A VESSEL USED BY HIM"

PD did not attend any ceremonies, banquet dinners, or "marches for life." She would tell me that too much attention would be on her and not God, which is not what she wanted. PD only wanted to be seen as a vessel used by Him.

Our Rachel stayed with us for around eighteen months and then married a young man she had met at her workplace. I had the honor of giving her away on behalf of her father. Rachel settled in upstate New York and now has five children and several grandchildren. David grew up all boy and became a Marine, served his country, and is now married with children of his own and working in upstate New York. Rachel was followed by eighty-seven other girls who were in need of support, love, and mentorship, which PD provided to all of them. Some of these girls were picked up in the middle of the night, one from a juvenile detention center, and on it went. They came to her in all different circumstances and backgrounds. They came hurting, scared, confused, lonely, and felt abandoned, and without love.

In PD, they found the love of God extended to them; she was someone who cared for them, believed in them, and encouraged them to succeed in life. Too many of these girls who came from broken homes lacked an understanding of love. With PD, this was the first time some of the girls ever actually felt loved. Our second girl was Roni, who spoke at PD's funeral with passion.

For many of the girls, the time they spent with PD was the first time they felt truly loved. She never judged them or was critical but encouraged them. I knew an enormous amount of work was going on in this ministry, and I asked PD once how many of the girls received Jesus as Lord and Savior. She was at her desk writing when I asked. Without looking up, she just smiled. That said it all. Everyone came to the Lord through this ministry. It was only the beginning of what God burdened her with a few years before. Due to PD's strength of faith and humble beginnings, the work goes on today with established ministries in Central Florida. Daily, lives are changed and thousands of babies have been saved from abortion. It was just like she believed it would be! I stand in awe.

# 7

# BENEDICTION FOR A SAINT

*Judy, Theron, PD, Jared, Brandon, and Derek*

PD was the oldest of five children in her family. Her childhood was normal. She played a lot, went on family vacations, and her family celebrated life together. Her family moved to Central Florida while PD was in high school, and she told me how sad she was at leaving her school and friends in Georgia and how awkward she felt entering a Catholic high school in Florida as a transfer student. She quickly made friends and, as one of her classmates told me once, she was not only one of the cutest girls in the entire school but was the nicest to everyone in all grades. During high school, she had close girlfriends from her class and dated often.

As mentioned earlier, PD started to become quite ill and had to leave Florida State University to face years of hospitals, examinations, medical trials, and yes, pain. No one could have foreseen the life ahead of her. Surprisingly enough, she would have probably considered most of her life struggles as a blessing because they enabled her to know and love the God of the Universe in a much deeper, more personal way.

## TELLING SCARS

The lyrics in the popular song "Scars in Heaven," by the group Casting Crowns, attempt to describe having scars from a lifetime of wounds. PD had more than most. She knew God intimately, as few would ever experience. She had an intimacy and thanksgiving with God that she gained through her battle for life and death. She would often see the path of life God laid out for her to travel, a path least traveled by most. God revealed to PD a journey through the physical and emotional pains of loss of health, marriage, sons' separation, and a son's death. Through it all, her belief, trust, and faith in God never wavered. She was never bitter on her path but had an innate joy in her heart, knowing and loving God, and looked forward with great excitement to the day of being in His presence for all eternity. PD Tennyson had the innocence of a child, a purity of heart, a faith that could move mountains, joy, and love in her heart knowing Jesus as her Lord and Savior, and would give all she could so that others would know the joy of knowing Him.

She marveled at all of God's creation; at night, she would gaze at the stars, moon, and clouds, and smile at the beauty of it all. The animals were her best friends, and she would often tell me that God had a sense of humor in creating them as they were so funny to her. She saw their innocence and love. Caring for all His creation was important to her, as it mattered to God.

# IMPORTANCE OF A THANKFUL HEART

In His Sermon on the Mount, Jesus reminds us, repeatedly, that we should consider ourselves "blessed," and that we should "rejoice, and be exceedingly glad: for great is your reward in Heaven . . ." (Matthew 5–12). Still, many of us can hardly find time to tell our Lord we are thankful. That was not the case with our PD. She lived thankfulness. PD was grateful to God for each and every day she lived and was so thankful that He allowed her to live and see her children grow up and become good men. Each of her sons married well, and she was able to hold her first grandchild only minutes after she was born. PD had an authentic love and joy for each day God had given her on this earth. She knew God was in control. She trusted that nothing happened to her unless it first passed through the hand of God. Needless to say, I thanked God each day for the privilege and honor of allowing me to be her husband from the beginning, for all the years of our marriage, and even now and forever will.

## OTHERS BEFORE SELF

She could have had many things but chose only a love to serve and help others and honor God with her own life. From time to time in our lives, we may have had the opportunity to cross paths with someone who is just different, more unique than all others that we have ever known. Without knowing the details of their life, you know that the person is special, different from all the rest you have ever met.

In spite of difficult circumstances in their lives, these special people are somehow able to overcome and live joyful and vigorous lives. They seem to live for one reason only—that they would honor God in every way while here on earth. They also appear excited and look forward to the life to come in Heaven with their Lord through all eternity.

PD was one of those unique people as well; she was a treasure to others. To know her was to love her, and she was a bright light in a spiritually dark world. She loved the unlovable, the downtrodden, the lonely, and lost when their paths crossed. She had the spiritual gift of exhortation and impacted lives with the love of God. Her journey in life was not an easy one but a powerful one. She was a living witness of God's miracles in her life and of His love for her and all who call on His name. Scripture tells us in Jesus' words that:

*Blessed are the poor in spirit, for theirs is the kingdom of heaven. Blessed are those who mourn, for they will be comforted. Blessed are the meek, for they will inherit the earth. Blessed are those who hunger and thirst for righteousness, for they will be filled. Blessed are the merciful, for they will be shown mercy. Blessed are the pure in heart, for they will see God. Blessed are the peacemakers, for they will be called children of God. Blessed are those who are persecuted because of righteousness, for theirs is the kingdom of heaven.*

**Matthew 5:3–10**

*His master replied, 'Well done, good and faithful servant! You have been faithful with a few things; I will put you in charge of many things. Come and share your master's happiness!"*

**Matthew 25:23**

Welcome home to your heavenly home. PD, well done my good and faithful servant.

The Apostle James offers a clue: "Dear brothers and sisters, when troubles of any kind come your way, consider it an opportunity for great joy" (James 1:2, NLT).

Through watching PD suffer and live a life of agony, I learned a lot. I believe that when suffering and excruciating pain are indescribable, something profound takes place within an individual. I saw PD face the cold reality of where her hope really resides. I saw her cry out in a plea to her Creator and be met with the embrace of His arms of love. PD was touched by His healing hands.

Some people called upon to endure great suffering grow bitter and resentful while others become just the opposite. I believe authentic purity starts to inhabit a person who has been at death's door on several occasions. When the illness subsides, each new day becomes a gift and something to smile about. Their very souls are somehow purified. They know Christ and walk in the pleasure of His presence. Waking each morning becomes a joy. I often heard my wife PD pray, "Lord, if through my suffering, others are drawn to You, I count it as joy."

Crohn's disease—or ulcerative colitis—is an incurable, autoimmune disease. PD's brother, niece, and nephew all have the malady. However, PD had it the worst.

Shortly after we were married, PD's dear Doctor Bone told me that because of all the physical traumas her body had suffered, we would have to add ten to fifteen years to PD's actual age as far as her expected lifespan. During PD's last hospitalization, her body had to fight also against two heart valves that weren't working properly. (No doctor would operate since it was too fragile and dangerous.) Both of her kidneys had failed, and she also had been doing dialysis for over seven years.

This was a tough situation—even for that "brave little soldier who just wouldn't die." She became just too frail to be operated on after more than thirty operations. Then, on October 24, 2016, PD gave up her valiant, brave, good fight.

## PD Finally Finds Peace

Her passing in the hospital room was a peaceful one. The hospitalist advised me that her organs were shutting down. I was told by the emergency room doctor, who consulted with the primary care physician, that there was nothing more they could do for her, and that it was time to let her go.

I talked with a pastor from my church, and one was sent to the hospital. It was late in the afternoon when she departed this earth and bowed before the throne of God. She was welcomed to her eternal home.

I held her hand that afternoon and buried my face next to hers as she took her last breath; I left the hospital late, filled with emptiness. When I got home, I took a very slow walk alongside my home. A large brown butterfly flew a few feet in front of me as I slowly walked. It stayed ahead until I stopped and then, finally, it flew into the night.

I then sat in a chair on my front porch. I found myself watching another little butterfly perched on the screen; this one was quite tiny. He seemed to look at me with his twitching little head. Instinctively, I knew it was PD. That little butterfly stayed there with me a long time, and I even talked to it as if it were PD. I touched the screen and held my finger there for what seemed like a long time. Eventually, it flew away and I got out of my chair.

I believe that God sent me a sign that it was her and she was with Him, reassuring me. A butterfly is a symbol of "new beginnings." I also recently learned that butterflies don't fly at night because it is the sun that energizes them and enables them to fly. Both my butterfly encounters happened, oddly, late at night on the eve of her passing.

Please understand that butterflies played no small part in our Tennyson home. There are paintings and sculptures of butterflies all over our home. I cannot but believe that a supernatural event took place that night. It was God's way of comforting me by saying she was with Him. A butterfly painting even hung over the bed where PD slept. I know it was both a visit and a message to me.

A few days later, at the cemetery, as I stood next to her grave and as the coffin was being lowered, I heard someone say, "Kevin, look at the butterfly flying over us." I looked and saw, once again, the identical large butterfly that flew in front of me several nights before!

This past year, in September 2021, I attended my granddaughter's wedding in Montana. The ceremony was held at a ranch next to the Flathead River and the beautiful Rocky Mountains. With this backdrop, it was a very beautiful and serene wedding with many friends and family there to witness and celebrate. I escorted the bride's mother as well as my great-granddaughter. I was seated next to the youngest of my great-grandchildren, who is named after PD, and what a beautiful little princess she is.

As the ceremony began, a large white butterfly flew down the center of the aisle and landed perfectly on my granddaughter's shoulder. It was like a kiss from heaven to remind us that PD is still with us. Her legacy continues, carried by the gentle flutter of a passing butterfly.

# End

# ABOUT THE AUTHOR

War time Navy veteran, Kevin Tennyson, currently lives in Florida. He found it an honor to care for and love his wife "PD." After her passing, he attributes *The Brave Little Soldier Who Just Wouldn't Die*, his first book, to the miraculous life of his wife, Patricia Diane Tennyson.

Her memory has both guided and comforted the author during the unspeakable tragedy of the loss of his wife, PD. It has also enabled him to find that peace that passes all understanding.

# HIGHLIGHTS OF THE BRAVE LITTLE SOLDIER

As our title suggests, the life experiences of one young lady were as devastating as being in the most severe form of military combat. But with the mental toughness of a combat Marine, and the unbelievable endurance of a saint, she overcame about as harsh a treatment as anyone could have endured, raising a family blessed with remarkable love and achievement.

Her story will have the reader saying, "You just couldn't make that sort of thing up." (Trouble is; this is not a story. Incredibly, it really did happen.)